THE FJH ADULT PIANO CURRICULUM BY

Jazz, Blues & Rags Treasures

Treasures

Volume 3 • Intermediate

THE F·J·H MUSIC COMPANY INC.
Frank J. Hackinson

Production: Frank J. Hackinson
Production Coordinators: Joyce Loke and Satish Bhakta
Art Direction: Terpstra Design, San Francisco, CA
Cover Art Concept: Helen Marlais
Cover Illustration: Marcia Donley
Engraving: Tempo Music Press, Inc.
Printer: Tempo Music Press, Inc.

ISBN-13: 978-1-56939-763-3

About the Series

Jazz, Blues, & Rags Treasures Volumes 1, 2, and *3* are devoted to ageless jazz, blues, and rag pieces for the adult piano student. The fine composers of this series were commissioned to create engaging original solos and arrangements. This series provides a perfect way for you to discover and enjoy well-known as well as new jazz, blues, and rag pieces. This series complements other FJH publications and is artistically strong, carefully leveled, and pedagogically sound. Have fun playing this wonderful repertoire!

Table of Contents

Royal Garden Blues

Clarence Williams and Spencer Williams   arr. Edwin McLean

FJH2036

Ragamuffin

Lee Evans

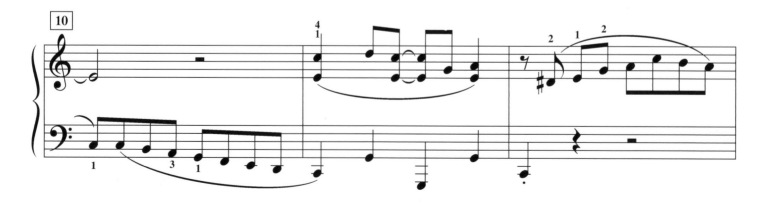

FJH2036

Chatterbox Rag

George Botsford   arr. Kevin Olson

Jazz Toccata

Martín Cuéllar

The Saint Louis Blues

William C. Handy   arr. Robert Schultz

Alexander's Ragtime Band

Irving Berlin   arr. Timothy Brown

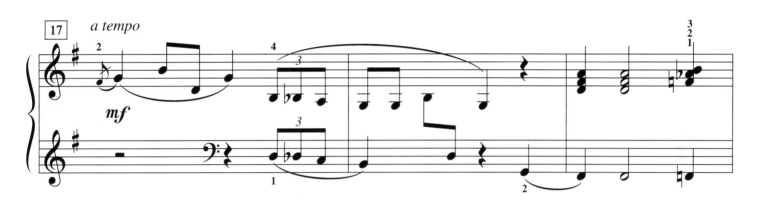

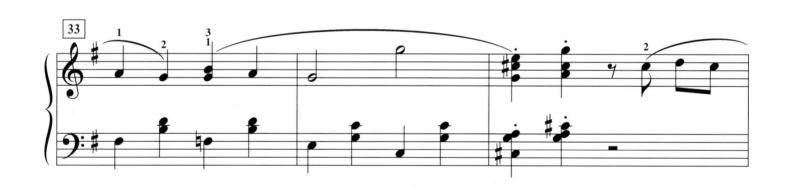

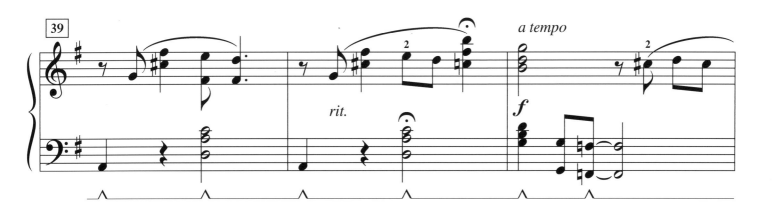

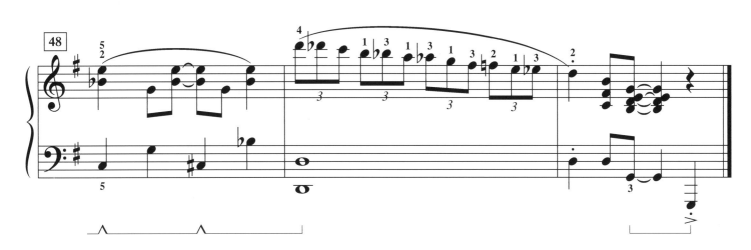

Angel Eyes

Music: Matt Dennis   Lyrics: Earl Brent   arr. Edwin McLean

The Memphis Blues

William C. Handy   arr. Kevin Olson

L.H. detached

ped. simile

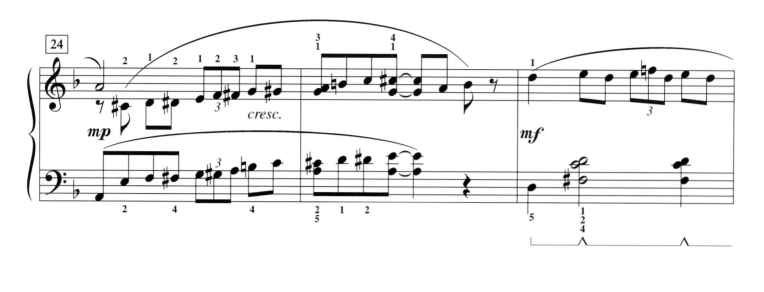

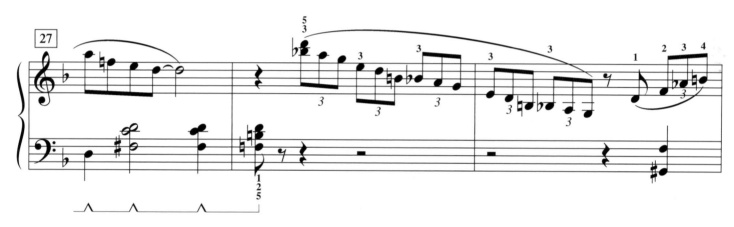

pedal as before

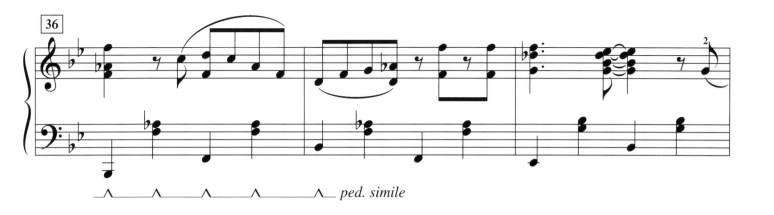

FJH2036

Wild Romantic Blues

Music: Jean Schwartz   Lyrics: Alfred Bryan   arr. Martín Cuéllar

Don't Say Goodbye

Edwin McLean

FJH2036

34

FJH2036

About the Pieces and Composers

Royal Garden Blues, by Clarence Williams and Spencer Williams

Clarence Williams wore many hats during the course of his life. He was a composer, jazz pianist, promoter, vocalist, publisher, and theatrical producer. He ran away from home when he was twelve years old to join a traveling minstrel show. By the time he was seventeen he had already founded his own publishing company, The Piron-Williams Publishing Company, with Armand J. Piron, a violinist, which, within a matter of a few years, became the one of the most successful publishing companies of its time.

The correct birth date for Spencer Williams is unknown as he gave different dates to different interviewers. Just like Clarence Williams, Spencer was known for being involved in various aspects of entertainment. He was a jazz and popular music composer, pianist, singer, actor, and director. He is considered to be one of the best African-American writers of popular songs.

Both writers were inducted into the Songwriters Hall of Fame in 1970.

Chatterbox Rag, by George Botsford

George Botsford was born in Sioux Falls, South Dakota, grew up in Iowa, and later moved to New York City to pursue his music career. He tried to create a new form of entertainment—miniature opera which was to be sung by about three or four people, but this form did not gain acceptance.

This piece in its original form is quite difficult to play. This arrangement has captured the flavor of the piece without compromising the sound. When you play this piece, does it remind you of any particular cartoon character who talks constantly?

Jazz Toccata, by Martín Cuéllar

Jazz Toccata was inspired by a letter to composer Martín Cuéllar from a teacher, asking him to write a new toccata with a jazz theme. This original solo piece relies on a continuous, moving pace to help create a bold, jazzy feel. It is the composer's wish that this piece will inspire students to experiment with new styles and themes.

The Saint Louis Blues, by William C. Handy

William C. Handy cultivated the controversial title "Father of the Blues" for himself since he believed, and rightly so, that he made a significant contribution to popularizing the "blues" form. Most of the information we have on Handy is from his autobiography, but significant research has been done on his life to substantiate the information.

His father and grandfather were ministers at Methodist churches in Florence, Alabama, and he was expected to follow in their footsteps. However, he showed interest in music early in his life, and eventually gained proficiency in playing the organ, piano, guitar, and especially the cornet and the trumpet.

Handy has been honored in various ways. A park on Beale Street in Memphis was named after him, a statue was erected in the park, a movie based on his life was released, and the U.S. Postal Office also issued a postage stamp in his honor. In addition, "Handys" (in 2006 they were renamed "The Blues Music Awards") are awards given annually to musicians for their contributions to blues music.

About the Pieces and Composers

Alexander's Ragtime Band, by Irving Berlin

Israel Baline, better known as Irving Berlin, started working early in life since his father passed away when he was very young. He did various odd jobs to support his family and it is said that he wrote his first song, for voice and piano, when he was working as a singing waiter. The owner of the café where he worked asked Berlin to compose an original song because a competing tavern had its own published song. So he co-wrote it with the café's pianist, Nick Nicholson. This song was published but his name was mistakenly spelt "I. Berlin" and this name stayed with him for the rest of his life.

Early in his music career he only wrote lyrics, however, circumstances forced him to start composing music as well. Since he was a self-taught pianist who could only play in the key of F sharp major, he bought a piano with a lever under the keyboard which helped him to transpose his songs mechanically.

Berlin was awarded the Grammy Lifetime Achievement Award in 1968.

Angel Eyes, by Matt Dennis and Earl Brent

Matt Dennis is an American songwriter, arranger, pianist, and singer. He was surrounded by music from a very young age and soon learnt to play the piano since his parents were vaudeville artists. He joined Horace Heidt's dance band when he was nineteen and since then played with various bands, composed and arranged music, many of which have been performed by Frank Sinatra, and was even a vocal coach to various band singers. Throughout his career, he has also appeared on TV and in movies.

Earl Brent was a lyricist whose most famous songs include *Angel Eyes*, *Let There Be Music*, and *Love is Where You Find It*.

They composed *Angel Eyes* which was first introduced in the movie, *Jennifer*, and this song has gone on to become a jazz and pop standard.

The Memphis Blues, by William C. Handy

Handy arranged an instrumental version of a folksong for the 1909 mayoral campaign of Edward H. Crump and titled it *Mr. Crump*. This song became a success and Crump went on to win the election. In 1912, Handy revised the same song, re-titled it, and published it as *The Memphis Blues*. The same year, Handy sold the rights to *The Memphis Blues* to a New York publisher, Theron A. Bennett Company, for only fifty dollars. This publisher added lyrics by George A. Norton to this piece and marketed it nationally to great success. Handy learned from this experience and went on to publish all his future works through his own publishing company.

About the Pieces and Composers

Wild Romantic Blues, by Jean Schwartz and Alfred Bryan

Jean Schwartz was born in Hungary and moved to the United States with his family when he was approximately ten years old. He continued with his music studies and for a while, worked at many non-musical jobs. He finally got a job as a pianist with a band and soon after, joined a prominent Tin Pan Alley publisher as a song plugger. Tin Pan Alley was the nickname given to the music print publishing industry, which was mostly based in New York from the late 19th century to the middle of the 20th century.

Alfred Bryan was a Canadian lyricist and songwriter who moved to the United States to work as a newspaper reporter. He is said to have written lyrics to over 700 songs, many of which, such as *Peg O' My Heart*, have become standards. He was inducted into the Songwriters Hall of Fame in 1970 and the Canadian Songwriters Hall of Fame in 2003.

Don't Say Goodbye, by Edwin McLean

Don't Say Goodbye is a lyrical jazz ballad with lush harmonies reminiscent of Bill Evans, a legendary jazz pianist who played on Miles Davis' famous album, *Kind of Blue*. This original solo piece is meant to be played in a lazy, slow, and lingering manner—always holding back the beat, never rushing forward. The ending should float away into nothingness.

About the Arrangers

Timothy Brown

Timothy Brown did his undergraduate studies at Bowling Green State University and received his master's degree in piano performance from the University of North Texas. His past teachers include Adam Wodnicki, Newel Kay Brown and Robert Xavier Rodriguez. He was a recipient of a research fellowship from Royal Holloway, University of London, where he performed his postgraduate studies in music composition and orchestration with the English composer, Brian Lock. He later continued his research at the well known Accademia Nazionale di Santa Cecilia in Rome, Italy.

His numerous credits as a composer include the first prize at the Aliénor International Harpsichord Competition for his harpsichord solo Suite Española (Centaur records). His recent programs include his original compositions showcased at the Spoleto Music Festival, and the Library of Congress Concert Series in Washington D.C. His recent commissions and performances include world premieres by the Chapman University Chamber Orchestra and Concert Choir, the Carter Albrecht Music Foundation, the Rodgers Center for Holocaust Education, and the Daniel Pearl Music Foundation.

Timothy Brown is an exclusive composer/clinician for The FJH Music Company Inc. (ASCAP)

Martín Cuéllar

Martín Cuéllar enjoys an active and successful career as performer, educator, clinician, and composer. He holds degrees in piano performance from the University of Texas at Austin (DMA, MM) and the Royal Conservatory of Music in Madrid, Spain (performance certificate) where he studied as a Rotary Scholar. Dr. Cuéllar has also conducted research and piano studies on the music of Enrique Granados at the Marshall Academy of Music in Barcelona (formerly the Granados Academy).

As a performer, Dr. Cuéllar has played concerts in the United States, Mexico, Brazil, Spain, Germany, and China. He is also nationally recognized as a composer of pedagogical piano pieces and is published by The FJH Music Company—publisher of not only his pedagogical compositions, but academic editions as well.

Dr. Cuéllar serves as associate professor of piano at Emporia State University in Emporia, Kansas.

Lee Evans

Lee Evans, professor of music and former chairperson of the Theatre & Fine Arts Department of Pace University in New York City, graduated from New York City's High School of Music & Art and completed degrees at New York University and Columbia University, receiving his Master of Arts and Doctor of Education from the latter. In addition to college level teaching, he also taught briefly at the junior and high school levels. Professionally, he concertized for ten consecutive seasons under the auspices of Columbia Artists Management, and has performed on some of the world's most prestigious stages, including the White House. He has been music coordinator/director for Tom Jones, Engelbert Humperdinck, Carol Channing, Cat Stevens, and Emerson, Lake, & Palmer. He is an acclaimed educator, performer, lecturer, composer, and arranger, and is author of over 90 published music books. Dr. Evans has worked to show it is possible for classical piano teachers with no prior jazz experience to teach jazz concepts with the same skill and discipline as classical music. Dr. Evans has succeeded in bringing an understanding of and feeling for jazz to keyboard students and teachers.

About the Arrangers

Edwin McLean

Edwin McLean is a composer living in Chapel Hill, North Carolina. He is a graduate of the Yale School of Music, where he studied with Krzysztof Penderecki and Jacob Druckman. He also holds a master's degree in music theory and a bachelor's degree in piano performance from the University of Colorado.

Mr. McLean has authored over 200 publications for The FJH Music Company, ranging from *The FJH Classic Music Dictionary* to original works for pianists from beginner to advanced. His highly-acclaimed works for harpsichord have been performed internationally and are available on the Miami Bach Society recording, *Edwin McLean: Sonatas for 1, 2, and 3 Harpsichords*. His 2011 solo jazz piano album *Don't Say Goodbye* (CD1043) includes many of his advanced works for piano published by FJH.

Edwin McLean began his career as a professional arranger. Currently, he is senior editor for The FJH Music Company Inc.

Kevin Olson

Kevin Olson is an active pianist, composer, and member of the piano faculty at Utah State University, where he teaches piano literature, pedagogy, and accompanying courses. In addition to his collegiate teaching responsibilities, Kevin directs the Utah State Youth Conservatory, which provides weekly group and private piano instruction to more than 200 pre-college community students. The National Association of Schools of Music has recently recognized the Conservatory as a model for pre-college piano instruction programs. Before teaching at Utah State, he was on the faculty at Elmhurst College near Chicago and Humboldt State University in northern California.

A native of Utah, Kevin began composing at age five. When he was twelve, his composition, *An American Trainride*, received the Overall First Prize at the 1983 National PTA Convention at Albuquerque, New Mexico. Since then he has been a Composer in Residence at the National Conference on Piano Pedagogy, and has written music commissioned and performed by groups such as the American Piano Quartet, Chicago a cappella, the Rich Matteson Jazz Festival, and several piano teacher associations around the country.

Kevin maintains a large piano studio, teaching students of a variety of ages and abilities. Many of the needs of his own piano students have inspired more than 100 books and solos published by The FJH Music Company Inc., which he joined as a writer in 1994.

Robert Schultz

Robert Schultz, composer, arranger, and editor, has achieved international fame during his career in the music publishing industry. The Schultz Piano Library, established in 1980, has included more than 500 publications of classical works, popular arrangements, and Schultz's original compositions in editions for pianists of every level from the beginner through the concert artist. In addition to his extensive library of published piano works, Schultz's output includes original orchestral works, chamber music, works for solo instruments, and vocal music.

Schultz has presented his published editions at workshops, clinics, and convention showcases throughout the United States and Canada. He is a long-standing member of ASCAP and has served as president of the Miami Music Teachers Association. Mr. Schultz's original piano compositions and transcriptions are featured on the compact disc recordings *Visions of Dunbar* and *Tina Faigen Plays Piano Transcriptions*, released on the ACA Digital label and available worldwide. His published original works for concert artists are noted in Maurice Hinson's *Guide to the Pianist's Repertoire, Third Edition*. He currently devotes his full time to composing and arranging, writing from his studio in Miami, Florida.